Not the ITSM Library

IT Service Management from Hell!

Based on Not-ITIL®

Brian Johnson
Paul Wilkinson

Editor, token woman and sanitizer: Annelise Savill

Dedication:
The very first Not-ITIL (Version 3) rip-off

This book is respectfully dedicated to the late Peter Skinner (who obtained the funds for the very first **** project) and to John Stewart (the true 'father' 'Godfather' or whatever of ****), a man of true humility and deep pockets.

Copyright and trademark policemen please note: every reference to 'Itil' in this book refers to the town of Itil. So there. Any references to the methodology of the same name is referred thus: ****.

This is (sometimes) a work of fiction; if after reading it you recognize yourself then maybe you take yourself too seriously.

Publishers Warning: The humour in this book was subject to extensive Teutonic Testing prior to release (no, honestly, it was). The Publisher read passages to volunteers from Bavaria, Westphalia and a number of Rheinlanders; sadly some injuries did result with numerous abdominal sutures being required. The 'funny' bits responsible for the injuries were, of course, removed (so were the sutures, eventually) to ensure a level of laughs commensurate with the needs of the people of Germany. So hold your sides and prepare for some serious Germanic japes and Teutonic titters a-plenty ...

Acknowledgements

Special thanks to itSMF (IT Service Management Forum) who continue to supply us with most of our ideas and material.

'This issue has arisen because you asked more than one person to look at the problem'

- itSMF January 2006

'Yesterday's hero is today's suspect. If you could fix it at 3 am when it broke, chances are you could have prevented it from breaking in the first place'.

- Ken Wendle – itSMF USA

Finally we would like to thank God: the Greatest Upgrader of them all. Who could have foreseen that all those Amoebae at the dawn of time could have gone through so many upgrades to result, finally in the human race? We humbly follow the principles of making our upgrade horrendously complex, significantly late (by about 1 billion years) and also generating a result that is no good to anyone or anything (and attempts to crash or destroy itself at any opportunity).

Concept and Text: Brian Johnson, Paul Wilkinson and Annelise Savill
Illustrations: Paul Wilkinson
Dutchman (needed to make this project deliver on time): Ivo van Haren
Anonymous Editing: Inform-IT

© 2006 Van Haren Publishing
First edition, first impression, January 2007
Publication date: much much much earlier than the official OGC V3 ****
Cover design and prepress: CO2 Premedia

Despite claims made in the text (largely for what passes as humour) the Authors and the Publisher are donating all royalties and a lump sum to support Macmillan Cancer Support.

WE ARE MACMILLAN.
CANCER SUPPORT

Contents

In Memoriam

This page is in Memory of all those whose career died as a result of not managing expectations. In other words of announcing or publicizing a launch of a new iteration, a new version, or a new contract before it is finalized or ready or agreed.

If you learn one thing from this book it is this: take advantage of all those unwanted e-mails and order whatever it takes to stop that premature exaggeration.

Foreword

In my defence, all Canadians are optimists and believers that the 'glass is half full -- not half empty'. This is the reason why I took on the task of being Chief Architect of ITIL V3. However, at times, the glass seemed to drain very rapidly and this is where a sense of humour (however dark) comes in.

When I was asked to draft a Foreword to this book I was delighted. Not only because I now have a deep pool of real life case-studies to use, but also because I think a sense of humour is sometimes the most important skill you can have when all you can see in your proverbial glass is sediment.

I recommend this book to you – read it when things seem really bleak and you'll find your life isn't half as bad as you thought.

The Publishers have promised me that they will remove all non politically-insensitive material from this version; so 'Goodbye' Token Woman; Goodbye Help Desk Neanderthal, Goodbye Token Frenchman and all those other unpopular stereotypes.......and goodbye derogatory comments about OGC and itSMF. I'm sure this will disappoint many of our previous readers, but as Chief Architect of ITIL® V3 I have my reputation to think of. ITIL® is growing up and so must we.

Enjoy the book!

Sharon Taylor
Chief Architect of ITL V3

(Ed: Sharon, sorry, but our Release Procedures went to cack and we forgot to take the stereotypes out. The released V3 product therefore contains a significant amount of bugs and other non-politically correct creatures. Also lots of derogatory remarks. We will rectify in future releases (or earlier if anyone fancies suing us).

Do as you would be done to;
only do IT first..........

The Cast of characters

Token Woman
'Hello again'

Help Desk Neanderthal
'What are you asking ME for?'

The Project Manager
I'm still in this book and intend to keep it that way

IT Professional
Still paid.....and so still in this book

User
...there are always users...

St Aidan – ancestor of Archbishop Aidan
Aim: To be the patron saint of all IT professionals. To manage the priesthood of Farquinell
Hobby: Visiting the flock. Often.

Introduction

In the new millennium the only way people make serious money is to re-introduce an existing product as a 'new version' which is uncannily similar to the previous version. Except it has a few more glitches. And doesn't interface with anything else any more.

We are not proud. If others can do it then so can we. But we're honest. If you've got the old version of '*IT Service Management from Hell*' then bin this book now and get a refund. This one isn't going to say anything different nor add any great new insights. It's just going to make the Author and Publisher more money out of you lot.

Like everyone else, we've generated this new upgrade using classic 'Best Practice'. We've appointed a Chief Architect (we love our titles, they just add the right level of humility to ripping off the general public) (we have to stop putting things in brackets, personally, we blame our parentheses) and we are proud to announce 'V3' of '*IT Service Management from Hell – based on Not ★★★★*'.

Not what? You may well ask. But first ask if the Chief Architect has new business cards. We have. That was the first and obviously the most important step. It is very important to have 'Chief' somewhere in your *curriculum vitae*. Ask Geronimo.

'My name is Geronimo and I have a Reservation'

Same is true, of course, of the original and version two ★★★★ series and anything else not 'architected' or better still, 'chief-ed'. An architect, particularly a Chief, can rip-off anything and being a Chief, it will be much more important than the stuff it was ripped off from. *(Ed: we put this line in after Sharon read the proofs...)*

We draw your attention (humbly, of course) to the new worst practice in this volume and apologize both for ripping off past icons and for not being Chiefs in the past.

In keeping with events, the *IT Service Management from Hell* team has decided to seek bids for the IPR of Not-****. Innovative solutions for ripping-off customers, getting money for doing nothing and maintaining a pretence of even vaguely wanting to do anything about Not-**** is not as important as guaranteeing piles of money. We will be listed on e-BAY very soon.

1

If you want to get anywhere don't start from here...

'Farquinell': mantra and cry of those lost in the **** wilderness: refers to sought after mystical magical place 'Where in the Farquinell are we?'

What is 'IT Service Management from Hell based on Not-**** V1 and V2' about then (and why do we need an upgrade?)

The second part is easier to answer than the first.

We don't need an upgrade – V1 and V2 are fine and, in our opinion, still pretty funny. What we do need is a) more money and b) the chance to incorporate all the new jokes we've been thinking about over the past three years. The content of V1 and V2 were pretty far-fetched, but in our wildest imaginations we couldn't have anticipated the events of the last three years. So, like a star, the upgrade was born.

So back to the 'what is Not-**** about then?'

To do this we have to look at the deep origins of **** …

1.1. ITIL-- origins

Little known true fact: Amazingly enough there was actually a place called Itil.

The capital of the state of Khazaria, Itil, lay on the river of the same name. The Khazars were a Turkic people, made up of tribes from the lower Volga and the Caucasus. As the power of the Rus grew, Khazaria came under threat. In the 960s AD, a prince of Kiev, Svyatoslav, went on a campaign to win territory from his neighbors, and sacked Itil and other Khazar cities. Within fifty years the Khazar Khanate had been destroyed.
(The associated priesthood of 'Farquinell' was rumored to have taken its name from the cries of pilgrims, looking for the lost city of Itil. "Where in the Farquinell is it …?" they would cry.)

Today, in the place of the early medieval Khazars' capital Itil, there is a town Astrahan, inhabited by about 500,000 people. It is the capital of Astrahanian District, a big port and (this is the important bit) an important railway junction. With the exception of a small display cabinet in a local museum containing excavations findings from the times of Kagnat, unfortunately there is no other trace of the town of Itil.

The river Itil, in the ancient times Rha, today is called the Volga. From its source in Waldaj to the Caspian Sea it is 3,530 km long, and it is still the longest river in Europe. Volga's basin is 1,360 km long, and its main side streams are Kama and Oka. Although it is a basin, it has no soap dish. Or buffalo. 'Volga' is, of course, what St Aidan, (the Patron Saint of IT Calamities) cries when he reads any of our 'Not' epics. St Aidan is an ancestor of the current Archbishop Aidan.

St Aidan the Lawmaker

St Aidan the Lawmaker did not exist until a case study was created in a management training class that was for some reason called 'Project New Zealand'. St. Aidan came into being and for some equally obscure reason was adopted as the patron saint of the priesthood of 'Farquinell'. Then for some even more obscure reason, St Aidan was given a beard and a flock of talking sheep as followers.

As in the old adage, they flocked about an awful lot and some of the followers were often required to flock off after particularly boring gatherings.

St Aidan was eventually brought into full existence because his flock believed in him so completely, even though his flock, of course, was in itself also a concept in a case study. Thus faith has since been used to prove the existence of higher beings. Such as Sting, or Bono.

Once made corporeal, St Aidan went about filling the coffers of the priesthood, pausing only to rack up a record number of space miles in his quest to visit every bar in every country around the globe. St Aidan took a flock of sheep with him wherever he went, giving rise to speculation that certain sheep were on more than friendly terms, an accusation denounced from the pulpit on many an occasion.

St Aidan and the ITILites

We include these facts simply to provide most of our readers with a vaguely interesting topic of after-dinner conversation at their next itSMF chapter meeting. The Not-**** V3 editors are now organizing an annual event at Astrahan where the highlight will be a visit to the aforesaid small display cabinet.

...we've come to claim 15 years of royalties or we sue.....
No, or we start chopping off the egos

The big lesson here is, of course, that the very first Itil disappeared without a trace because the town hadn't had an upgrade in a very long time. No matter how good your product (or town) is, your customers soon get bored and will go elsewhere. The only way to keep your product going is to make your customers life hell by giving them an upgrade. Then they'll be far to busy sorting out the mess you've left them with to look for alternatives, or look for neighboring tribes to pick a fight with.

Another lesson is that no matter how big you are now, you're not too big to disappear.

On another point, we note that the Dutch have joined up with the Khazars to have the copyright to the title Itil re-instated to its original owners. It will soon be displayed in the small display cabinet in the local museum.

1.2 The Creation of today's ****

The big mistake that the original town of Itil made was to forget to put a little ® beside the town name. This meant that nearly 1,000 years later, the British Government in the guise of the CCTA was able to use the age old colonial tactic of deploying its not insignificant elite IT crack forces to take the name.

So the British Government adopted the name. But not the pronunciation. Today you'll find the Americans pronounce it 'eye'-til and the Brits 'it'-til. The official site says there is not right or wrong in the pronunciation. But, of course, we know better. It is, in fact, the Volga dialect which means that it is pronounced like none of the above, but we're not going to tell you until we've got it copyrighted.

The very first **** was quite a small project whose aim was simply:

the creation of a non money-spinning, altruistic venture based on documenting things that people are either already doing or should be doing. And itSMF.

But to do this they had to create 'a project'. And no one knew how to do projects then. And so Frankenstein's monster was born and it was called PRINCE. But unfortunately PRINCE is a rather well established tobacco brand in the Netherlands and Scandinavia and so this name didn't last long (remember the lesson about the original town of Itil ...?) So the crafty CCTA crack troops added a number to it and trademarked it (and so PRINCE2® was born ...). The interesting thing here is that it wasn't called PRINCE1. Clearly this method had an upgrade even before the first edition was released. We are particularly impressed with this approach. Essentially ... this is the product formally known as PRINCE.

This was all far too easy. And so, the British Government (CCTA), to justify their salaries and demonstrate their reputation of turning any project into a hopeless IT project disaster created the itSMF. In theory the itSMF is to provide a forum of like-minded souls to discuss and get the best practice principles established. The problem here is the 'like minded souls' bit. As anyone in a room of IT Service Managers will know, they can discuss minutiae until the cows come home (or the alcohol runs out) – or in fact until the cows have been repackaged as hamburgers. And then the British Government crowned the whole project off by inviting the ultimate fiendish disputants to join the table - the Dutch.

And so the stage was set for the greatest British export product since we started up our little project in Australia and staffed it with our finest personnel. Hell, even Microsoft bases much of its empire in it (****, not Oz). To cap it all, we acknowledge that while everyone else on the planet would have made enough out of this to buy a small country, or at least a decent sized atoll, the British government have missed most of the commercial opportunities – in fact, their own rules forbid them even to get even a meal out of it.

> **This follows a fine British precedent and tradition of inventing really great sports – and then being completely hopeless at them.**

1.3   **** and Upgrades

The decision to upgrade **** was made such a long time ago that references go back to biblical times. (Lets face it, God clearly appointed Job his 'project resource': if anyone can't see that the whale is a euphemism for PRINCE2 they need their head examining).

EXTRACT FROM THE BOOK OF ST AIDAN VERSES 1-39

LET US GO FORTH AND ASK OF THE WORLD WHAT THEY WANT IN VERSION THREE OF THAT WHICH IS KNOWN AS THE BOOKS OF '****' (THAT WHICH CANNOT BE SPOKEN ALOUD WITHOUT ADDING ˜ OR ˙, NEVER MIND BEING IMPLEMENTED) AND THEN TELL THEM WHAT THEY CAN HAVE. LET US THEN BREAK BREAD WITH THE USUAL SUSPECTS AND MASSAGE UNTO THEM THEIR GIGANTIC EGO'S AND PROVIDE FOR THOSE THEIR DAILY OPPORTUNITIES TO JUMP ON THE GRAVY TRAIN THAT VERILY THEY BELIEVED HAD DEPARTED BEFORE THEY DECIDED TO GET ON BOARD AND PRETEND THEY HAD JUST MISLAID THEIR TICKETS AND WERE A BIT DELAYED BECAUSE THEY HAD TO LOOK FOR THEM, THEN THEY HAD FORGOTTEN TO CANCEL THE MILK AND BY THE TIME ALL THIS WAS SOLVED SEVEN YEARS HAD PASSED AND THEY SUDDENLY REALIZED, OH DEAR, WE BETTER GET THAT TRAIN BECAUSE OTHERWISE OTHER PEOPLE WERE MAKING LOOT HAND OVER FIST AND WELL, THEY MIGHT AS WELL HAVE SOME, AND IF THEY WERE QUICK THEY COULD MAKE A FEW QUID BEFORE THEY WERE FOUND OUT.

AND LO! THERE DIDST APPEAR A STAT (SORRY, A STAR) IN THE SKY THAT SPELT "MONEY".

AND YET DIDST THE PROPHETS OF THE NEW TESTAMENT OF '****' AT FIRST SHAKE THEIR HEADS AND SCRATCH THEIR GREY BEARDS AND TEAR ASUNDER THEIR UNDERWEAR FOR THEY DID DISCOVER THAT THE OLD TESTAMENT SPAKE TRUTH AND ONLY VERITABLE COCK-

UPS BY THOSE THAT SHOULD HAVE KNOWN BETTER
DIDST ALLOW CORRUPTION TO BE VISITED ON THE
LATER BITS. (THE BOOK OF IMPLEMENTING '****', THE
BOOK OF I DON'T SEE ICT (NOW A MAJOR FILM--- WHO
CAN FORGET THE LINE 'I SEE DUMB PEOPLE'), THE
BOOK OF APPLICATION MAYHEM, THE BOOK OF THE
IT PERSPECTIVE ON THE BUSINESS OF IT WHENCE
CONVOLUTED BY THOSE WHO WERE NEVER THERE IN
THE FIRST PLACE ... AND YET, HAVE WISDOM ENOUGH TO
CAST THEIR PEARLS. OR SOMETHING.)

THENCE DID THESE NEW AND NOT FALSE PROPHETS
(NOT FALSE; WE WISH TO UNDERSCORE THEIR
INTEGRITY) WITH HEAVY HEART AND SLIGHTLY LESS
ENTHUSIASM THAN BEFORE WHEN THE ASSEMBLED
DIDST THINK THEIR WALLETS WOULD RUNNETH OVER,
SAY UNTO THE WAITING MASSES "YEA VERILY THOUGH
THE FIRST BOOKS WERE NOT CREATED BY THE EGO'S
ASSEMBLED HERE, NEVERTHELESS AND UNFORTUNATELY
WE CANNOT FIND SUFFICIENT FAULT TO GET OUR
NAMES ON THE CORE BOOKS. BUT FEAR NOT, THE
CONGREGATION HEREIN HAS DISCOVERED THAT BY
CREATING COMPLEMENTARY GUIDANCE WE CAN ATTACH
THE '****' TRADEMARK AND THEREBY CLAIM THAT ALL
WISDOM IS OURS BECAUSE WE KNOW EVERYTHING AND
UNLESS **** IS MENTIONED NO ONE WILL BE FOOLED.
AND VERILY THIS SHALT MAKE OGC PILES OF DOUGH
EVEN THOUGH SINCE WAY BACK WHEN THEY HAVE SPENT
NOT A BEAN ON DEVELOPMENT."

LO! THE SONS OF ITSMF WILL, HOWEVER, RISE AND
OFFER MONEY TO THOSE THAT ARE DESIROUS OF
BOARDING THIS GRAVY TRAIN BEFORE THE WORLD
DOTH WAKE AND IDENTIFY A RIP-OFF. THEY SHALT
SELL AGAIN TO THE UNWISE AND THE GULLIBLE YET
AGAIN THE SAME **** THEY SOLD BEFORE, (THAT IS ****
OF COURSE, NOT '****', THOUGH ON OCCASION IT HAS
BECOME DIFFICULT TO TELL THEM APART).
THEY SHALT ALSO LAY CLAIM TO ANY MENTION OF
THE LETTERS '****' BECAUSE IT HAST NOW BECOME TOO
IMPORTANT TO ALLOW MERE MORTALS TO MENTION
AND NOT, OF COURSE, BECAUSE MONEY IS AT STAKE. THE
PROPHETS OF THE 'NEW TESTAMENT' WILL GO FORTH
AND TELL THE WORLD OF THEIR GENIUS AND HOW THEY
DIDST BEGET EVERYTHING IN THE FIRST PLACE.
AMEN.

2

Get on with it ..... What about Upgrading Best Practice?

**Computers make very fast,
very accurate mistakes**

So after you have decided that you really need an upgrade the next stage is to deploy PRINCE2 and create as many committees as possible. If these committees are international and justify a jet-setting life style so much the better. Seekers after truth and any idea of how to begin are referred to any of the following country case studies. The case studies are, of course, meaningless unless you are the sort who copies the exam answer from the student alongside, but nonetheless, they are recommended because we get paid.

> ## Case Study: Not **** V3 Upgrade
>
> We followed this policy with Not **** V3 Upgrade: Our editors and Sharon could show the UN a thing or two, because we managed to distil (there's that glass of international lubricant again) some sense out of the contradictory feedback and input from people from 15 different countries. And then we got consensus.

The million dollar question is how do you get consensus from such a wide and disparate group of people? This is where readers are advised to copy the following Best Practice approach: the St Aidan Approach to Diplomacy (SAAD).

This is based on a few fundamental principles, and a deep and sensitive understanding of what makes people tick (especially the Dutch):

Principle 1
Accept that the Dutch are going to have thought about, discussed, written, QA'd and finally published the material before everyone else has even got the first Project Board meeting in the diaries (*Ed: Note the Dutch avoid PRINCE2 where they possibly can*).

Principle 2
Ask the French for their input at about 12.30. This is lunch time and so they'll have better things to do than consider boring IT concepts.

Principle 3
DON'T ask the French, Belgians or the French Canadians anything at the same time or in the same room. If you make this mistake a) be sure to have a first aid box, and b) shove your project plan back two years.

Principle 4

Don't invite anyone from the Antipodes to a conference call in the afternoon, European time. They'll be half asleep even if they've managed to get the alarm clocks set, or persuaded their probation officers to allow the call in the first place …

Principle 5

Make the Americans the last on the list and tell them it was all their idea in the first place. Also, pretend to be Irish.

Principle 6

Apply for copyright from the Egyptians because they have finally run out of patience that their pyramids® are forever getting ripped-off in **** books as the basis for yet another useless diagram.

Principle 7

Publish everywhere but China - which has more certified (whatever that is) individuals than all the other nations added together. Also fewer mandarins than the British civil service or your local greengrocer, and the only nation where pirate books and Microsoft applications can be ordered from a numbered menu suspended above the receptionist desk in Beijing airport.

Principle 8

Ensure that the New Zealanders have been consulted on at least 112 occasions, ideally in 112 different countries, prior to doing anything at all, even thinking about anything. And that means anything.

The final element of SAAD is a beard. This makes even potentially long meetings very short as there is only so long you can bear looking at one. It is to the detriment of ****V3 that Sharon drew the line at this one and we seriously question her dedication here.

Tom is trying to get his new computer working. He's having trouble so he calls over Harry to give him a hand. Harry switches on the computer then asks Tom if he wants it password protected. "Oh yes, I read about that in the manual. I think the password I'll have is 'DaffyDuckBugsBunny TomandJerry'." "That's a very long password," says Harry "Yes," replies Tom. "But the manual says it has to be at least four characters."

3
The Development Stage

Someday, the people who know how to use computers will rule over those who don't. And there will be a special name for them - secretaries.

3.1 Development Stage 1: Defining a standard glossary

In order to do a proper upgrade you've just got to be talking the same language.

IT Babble

You cannot tempt us on this one; to be specific, not even for money. Well, for money, of course, we can be tempted. (That was what is technically called a lie.)

Anyway, only the highest paid consultants can converse fluently in IT Babble. An arcane dialect of mysterious origin, Babblers enable the smooth running of the ITSM world.

IT Babble and the source of the greenhouse effect - calculation

Calculate the weight of carbon dioxide exhaled by every speaker who ever got on their hind legs at any event in the last 10,000 years and told you what to do. Then add the weight of the oxygen they consumed producing the CO_2. Then divide by the volume of gaseous intake requirements of the audiences and the square root of the weight of the likely mixture of lethal gases expelled into the already noxious air following an overdose of pale ale and vindaloo on Brighton seafront.

Finally subtract the age of St. Aidan and you will discover that IT Babble has been proven to cause the greenhouse effect. And that is only the good things it has caused. When did you last align your business with IT based on what someone told you at a conference?

Unlike most languages the IT Babble glossary doesn't evolve – it regresses. And you know we're right. Perfectly normal young people starting their career in IT are capable of the basics of conversation and know what to do with facial hair. But, as their career moves on, language descends into a state where words are replaced firstly by three letter acronyms (TLAs) and then, later, by meaningless grunts, as they huddle over yet another addictive computer software package:

Hello	Grunt
How are you?	Yawn
How may I help you?	Belch
May I talk to a real human being?	Skype me

We want to know if the Americans will agree to restrict ITIL bullshit emissions...

KYOTO AGREEMENT

Can we have a face to face conversation?

I only talk to people when I can look at my in-box and correspond at the same time

Do you realize you're being rude?

Where's the log off button on this person?

You will find that the IT Babble Glossary in Not V3 is completely different and incompatible with the Glossary found in V1 and V2. The full list is supplied in an Annex to this book. If we presented you with something easy to understand then you wouldn't need an upgrade would you?

"IT Service Management from Hell" has this to say about Common Glossaries

IT Babble began many years ago at the beginning of the universe when people weren't yet busy even thinking about the concept of computers, let alone how they could be used to download porn or confuse people. IT Service Management didn't exist. Yes, it is hard to imagine a universe without it. But try. As such there was, at that time, no need for IT technoids. The grunting Neanderthal technoid we have come to know and love and adopt as our role model wasn't even a twinkle in his mother's eye.

However, the universe wasn't devoid of all types of low life organisms. They still had Consultants. Next to slimy swamp crawling life forms and brainless single cell creatures there existed Consultants. After all, which bright spark advised The Almighty Industries Ltd. about creating the world in seven days? It must have been a Consultant. Consultants would sit around for days, months, years just pondering, wondering about their right to exist. Why were they born? What was their purpose in life? They hadn't yet realized that their sole right for existence, the computer, hadn't yet been invented and wouldn't be invented for millions of years.

With all that time to pass they had to come up with something. They would sit around drawing models on cave walls for each other and would spout on in grunts to each other their latest theories on … on … just about anything that anybody was willing or usually unwilling, to listen to. Surprisingly enough it was probably Consultants who were responsible for the rapid adoption of language and the ability of humans to speak to one another. They realized that grunting to each other wasn't getting them anywhere, besides which, they could all grunt the same grunts which meant they couldn't differentiate themselves from their rivals, other than beating the excrement out of them. They needed to find a way of creating a form of differentiated grunting. As such they sat around trying to dream up buzzwords and eventually formed sentences around them. One of the earliest buzzwords they invented was 'leverage' which they have all been using as a mark of respect ever since, whereas one of the first words ever spoken by the technoids millions of years later was 'bollocks' which shows how subtly we have evolved. Anyway, getting back to Consultants.

As we said, Consultants would spout on endlessly to each other. One day, one of the Consultants was doing what Consultants did then … still do … when one of the audience, having suddenly seen the light, said basically, "put a sock in it!". However, because socks hadn't yet been invented this came out as "put a fish in it", which was a polite way of asking him to stop. Consultants being slow creatures and not easily switched off when in full verbal swing, this Consultant did what all consultants do: he smiled politely and carried on.

What happened next is not written down, as the recorded minutes were shredded, rumours being that one of the Consultants who was developing accounting tendencies thought it a bad idea to keep records of anything incriminating and fed the tasty evidence to a passing brontosaurus.

Anyway, a large fish was stuffed in the mouth of the Consultant to shut him up.

The audience cheered as the person holding the fish declared "That will stop him babbling" and the fish was quickly named the 'babble' fish.

Millions of years passed and the story was passed on from generation to generation. What started out as a fish that was called a "babble fish" that was stuffed into somebody's mouth to stop them spouting bullshit and nonsense later became translated as a 'babel fish' that was put in your ear to help you make sense of any language, even ****"

And just to prove that even after history makes the same point again and again we STILL don't learn, we note that the original concept of Babel Fish was NOT copyrighted in time. This means that YET AGAIN someone else has made off with a perfectly good idea and made an absolute mint out of it. Now come on everyone ... even Paris Metropole has caught up with this idea. Can we all pay attention!

3.2 Development Stage 2: Quality Process -- Plan Do Check Act

The Deming Quality Circle is all about delivering upgrade after upgrade of good stuff. It's great because it has no beginning and no end: just a continuous cycle of repeating the job again and again. Inspired by the legend of Sisyphus, it is not for nothing that the famous diagram looks like a hill and the Plan Do Check Act wheel looks like the infamous rock the poor sod had to keep on rolling up that hill.

Anyway to get your Upgrade really pukka, follow these simple rules:

Plan: Plan how the upgrade will cause you the least amount of effort but raise the most amount of money

Do: In other words how you 'do' the customer. This stage reaches completion when the customer yells 'I've been done!'

Check: This refers to how much you are billing the customer

Act: Fast. Get out while you can. If your customer is a Bank move out of US and to the UK. The British would rather lose millions than sue and look stupid; the Americans – well we all know the answer to that one.

'What does the DO stand for?
.....Simple DO unto the Users
before they DO unto you.'

3.3 Development Stage 3: Chief Architects Prayer

At this point your upgrade project will, no question, be going 'tits-up' (this description is appropriate because your token woman will, of course, be taking all the blame here …).

This is where the following prayer, to whichever God or gods you worship, will help:

'GOD GRANT ME SERENITY, TO ACCEPT THE THINGS I CANNOT UPGRADE, COURAGE TO UPGRADE THE THINGS I CAN AND THE WISDOM TO KNOW THE DIFFERENCE'

'And this is where 'our successful project' turns into 'your project disaster', Frances'

At this point you need someone to actually do the Upgrade. Firstly to actually get the job done and secondly to blame for all the screw-ups.

This person is always called the Project Resource. You will know you've found him if a) he is an **** Foundation certificate and b) he has a photo of St Aidan the Patron Saint of IT Calamities on his wall. Next to his Scott Adams Calendar. And his poster of Buffy the Vampire Slayer.

'Am I to assume things aren't going according to your planning?'

How many programmers does it take to change a light bulb? None. That's a hardware problem.

4

Drafting the Upgrade

I wish I had learned Latin at school and then I could have been able to converse better in Latin America

(Dan Quayle)

4.1   Process for Defining the Upgrade

OK this is the easy part. To look really good, tell the Customers they need some Consulting and that you and other industry experts, advisors and other specialists who have either been on the gravy train for a long time and depend upon it for food or power, and ideally both, or those who can spot a good bandwagon and are going to jump aboard irrespective of public good or any sense of shame, and will introduce them to like-minded individuals.a

Then have a look at holiday brochures and find experts in the places you've never been before. Select a bunch of sycophants and arrange to meet in a professional venue (Las Vegas is good, Birmingham and Brighton lack something....)

Then spend 6 months writing up your finding and releasing those findings in extremely pompous forums.

Case Study – It Service Management from Hell V3 Upgrade

To massage our egos good and proper we went out to countries around the world to find sycophants that we could use. More than one country was visited and nearly one person declared interest and told us what to do with *IT Service Management from Hell based on Not-*****

Unfortunately, anatomical dysfunctions prevented that happening, so we came up with just telling you what you were going to get anyway, since we had already decided that we were the smartie-pants.

First we were keen to recruit a Stakeholder who had heard of 'IT Service Management from Hell' but until the money rolled in, had no interest. Our Publisher kindly volunteered for this role.

Then we decided that our core guidance, *IT Service Management from Hell V1 and V2*, were not going to change. Not because they were that brilliant mind you; mainly because even we recognized we could not sell the same books again without kicking up a bit of a stink.

Instead we came up with a truly brilliant concept of rewriting the books that were rubbish.

Of course we then changed our minds and decided to change everything anyway so that you would have to buy everything

---

and we could show how clever we are. Whether you like it or not.

Also, we decided to provide templates and models that would enable those who are so intellectually challenged that they cannot spell 'SLA' or 'plan' to be able to fill-in the blanks of a template that their managers will just die laughing at, thereby ensuring we get consultancy assignments later. Additionally, of course, we will get money from providing this rubbish, but hey, we are capitalists.

And erm, did we mention the rubbish? We are going to shift that into 'complementary guidance' so if the **** hits the air conditioning (that is **** not '****') we can say it was not really Not −****. A sort of Not Not-**** we suppose.

Oh yes, and we would attempt to portray that we are innovative by pretending that 'industry verticals' can apply. Since Paul, the author, has lived in Holland for years and is well known in pharmaceutical circles, he is responsible for guidance in this sector. As a Sunderland supporter, Brian, the other author, knows only too well the value of a good foundation to teamwork, so he is now 'sports complementary guidance guru' and has negotiated the inclusion of the Not-**** Foundation exam in this book (see Annex A).

Technoids is vacant. (Should that be 'are vacant'? Ed.) No, it is plural. Like staff is. Though they are vacant in another sense.

Sharon will be our conscience, and the still, small voice of calm. But as we all know; no one listens to common sense, and, together with being the new 'token woman', she really had no hope.

Aaahhh, good times.

5

Release of Draft for Review

Email to IT department:
CanYouFixTheSpaceBarOn-
MyKeyboard?

5.1 Feedback stage

This is the stage when everyone who gave you the feedback for change in the first place now tells you they liked the original version instead.

But they miss the point.

The point is to make money – not whether the new version is any good or not.

We secretly follow the God principle here: hell, who did she ever QA her upgrades with? (But there again, you could argue – it shows)

So NOT **** best practice is to follow this principle and make the Review as token as possible with the aim of getting no comments in at all. Try the following tactics based on the previously tried scoping exercise:

Principle 1
Ask the Dutch to run the review. They will have sent out, received comments, upgraded, change controlled and have had a pint and a-----erm herbal cigarette, all before anyone has managed to access the e-mail in the first place.

'itSMF NL ('Bad van Bon') prepares for V3 QA Audit'

Principle 2
Ask the French to make their comments in English. Guaranteed they will still be sulking in a year's time – and won't send any comments back.

Principle 3
Tell the Canadians that you've asked the French. The Canadians won't reply either.

Principle 4
Tell the British you are looking for European feedback. They'll automatically assume you don't mean them and not bother to reply.

Principle 5
Send review to the Americans in the last week of November.

6

Final V3 Release and Publication

Animal testing is cruel; they get nervous and confused and give the wrong answers

We can only refer to the Kings of Upgrades and New Releases -- Hollywood. Well known for making millions by re-hashing the same old story we believe that they have mastered Best Practice to a level which cannot be surpassed.

6.1 Blockbusters!!

You can learn a lot from the Hollywood movie moguls and it would appear that IT companies worldwide already have. How so, you ask?

The moguls have been quick to spot a winning film formula and turn it into repeat business and, of course, a lot of money. The first of these that we can remember was probably the 'Rocky' series of movies. We can't even remember how many it was! Four or five? Probably about the same number as the IQ of the leading actor.

And what about the Star Wars films? *'May the force be with you'* was the catchphrase of the time.

More recently we have had Harry Potter, existing in a world of reality and a world of magic and fantasy. Another battle between good and evil ...and what about Lord of the Rings? Ugly, slimy creatures of the underworld that want to dominate us and take everything we have ... a magic ring that everybody seeks to give them power over all.

What has all this got to do with IT Service Management?

Owners of **** have seen the success in the formula and has created '****', '****' version 2 and soon to be released '****' version 3. It's that winning formula of Hollywood!! And the similarities run deep:

The films seem to get more spectacular and dazzling all the time, whetting our appetite for more. We can hardly wait for the next film (actually *we can* wait, but the Box Offices tell a different story, until the punters realize that recycling is not revitalizing). One thing that **** doesn't have that the Hollywood blockbusters does, is some sort of catchphrase or sexy sounding subtitle to get you going. We believe these are called 'hooks'. We have decided to help out by providing a few 'hooks' for ****.

'**** change IT for ever"
'**** make you think again'
'**** never be the same again'
'**** be your worst nightmare come true'

	Hollywood	****
****	Rocky: a series of films about somebody beating his adversary senseless. It was messy, bloody and there was a lot of suffering and promises, and hopes not fulfilled.	**** a set books that was turned into bureaucratic procedures for beating the users into submission. **** was applied poorly, it was messy. There was a lot of frustration and confusion and the promises and hopes were not fulfilled.
**** V2	Star Wars: May the force be with you. A battle of good against evil. An environment of high technology. Leaping across time and the universe..	**** as a *de-facto* standard. The business and IT dilemma and the business perspective books. The introduction of the Infrastructure Management book. An international explosion of **** and the itSMF. Countries seemingly in a time warp and suddenly discovering **** 10 years later.
**** V3	Harry Potter A world of reality and magic and fantasy. A battle between good and evil. A magic ring that everybody seeks to own, to give them power over all. Ugly, slimy creatures of the underworld who want to dominate us and take everything we have.	The reality of poor IT performance and the magic wand of IT governance to create the fantasy of business and IT alignment. The continual struggle of business and IT. The pervasive nature of IT and the promise of IT as a business differentiator, offering a competitive edge if only we can bring IT under control. IT Governance and all that hype has given new power to the consultancy firms. They want to dominate us with their promises of compliance and take away our money by charging ridiculously high rates for helping us.
**** in general	The chance to sell the same story in new packaging and make more money.	The chance to sell the same story in new packaging and making more money.

Send your tips to the Office of Galactic Commerce for sexy new catchphrases for ****.

And finally the Office of Galactic Commerce will probably adopt Harry Potter as the **** mascot. With a wave of his magic **** wand, all the problems facing IT organizations will vanish once and for all. A new Catch phrase "****AMUNDO"!!

7

Preparing the V3 Release
for Market

Can you identify which word includes all the vowels in order? Or are we just getting facetious?

7.1 Industry verticals

If you really want to make money than make sure your upgrade is relevant to the following industries.

Entertainment

Seeing as how girls can drink way more than men (and hold it better) who better than your chief-ette to explain how Not-**** is applied to the drinking persons sector:

Well, if you have nine pints (or incidents as we prefer to call them) this definitely will add up to be a problem.

Almost certainly (unless you are a proper northerner) your capacity will have been reached and it is likely you will want to create an emergency change and skip right into release management.

If you have not processed the request through your numbed brain cells, then you might well find that your release has been unfortunately timed and another change (at best underwear, perhaps also trousers) has to be scheduled.

Of course, if these items are not available it is a breach of many things, never mind any waste of space SLA, and it is likely that a night in the cells and a large fine may well have an impact on your finances.

Add to that the unexpected cost of failing to budget for the outage and well, there you are. As the only female member of CamRSM, I am often asked to use my feminine wiles to get the authorities to drop the charges when colleagues have been banged-up overnight in Horseferry Road. Usually I don't bother.

CamRSM

The Campaign for Real Service Management (CamRSM) has been in existence ever since the itSMF was very small and operating out of the back of a Ford Anglia in Norfolk UK.

CamRSM membership is limited to those with a taste for real ITSM; none of that pussyfooting around with standards, frameworks and getting stuff right first time. As for repeatable, well, try a few pints of CamRSM favorite, Olde Breakwinde Ale and you will soon have a definition for the word.

Members of CamRSM are generally described as having beards, 'bought and paid for' beerguts and they meet in rather drafty venues to queue for solutions that have been developed using a pair of old tights and water sourced from companies run by venture capitalists who know what they are doing and buy the bottled stuff for their own consumption.

These CamRSM meetings are really boring. After years of research we guess that the Americans go because the meetings are booked in the Village Hall of Las Vegas or Long Beach or Disneyland. But we are still at a loss to explain why the Brits go to Brighton and Birmingham functions..........our best guess is that flocking followers of Farquinell like sticking together and Brighton and Birmingham give them ample opportunity to repeat the mantra 'Where in the Farquinell are we this year...?"

Not the itSMF Panel using all their skills to access the Conference hotel late night Adult channel......

Banks
Banks have money. '****' wants money. Ergo, '****' applies to Banks more than any other sector anywhere in the galaxy.

Use it to prop open doors and windows, or to plug those areas in the safe where no money has been placed, or just use it as toilet tissue; no matter what you do, it can only improve the environment.

And, of course, if you adhere to the directions in the way that only a bank can, you will be recognized as a right banker.

Pharmaceuticals
Actually, pretending that we know enough about 'industry verticals' to gain even the tiniest idea of how '****' might apply in different ways is certain to bring in rewards. So the same applies to Not-****. As experts on pharmaceuticals through living in the Netherlands for many years, we can explain clearly, consistently and without dribbling on, or going off the point or anything like that, we can focus on, well anything. For example, 'Intelligent Design'- there really must be an Almighty because if there wasn't how would you be able to explain '****'? It is so complicated that it can't have happened by accident, no matter what the government tells us, and whooaaaaaaaaaaaaaa, shooting star man, why don't we teach 'Intelligent Design' in

our classrooms along with the theories of evolution of '****'
over many versions. You can't prove it's not true, and nice beard
Aidan, is it yours? Or did you borrow it from the prophet David?
Either way the highlights just glisten like, like, like something, is
that coming round here again? Thanks man, whhhoooo-hah ,
high availability, that's what we were thinking of and that's why
you need whatever it is that we thought we could remember
before we left home this morning.

Manufacturing

Quality standards commonly apply to the manufacturing
industry. That is one reason you should work somewhere else. If,
however, called upon to apply Not-****, then consider raking
up the need to continuously improve, 'plan-do-check-act' and
so on, that will surely keep the door open until the check is
signed. If anyone mentions Six Sigma, nod wisely and claim that
you have at least seven, not including the ones you left in the
cupboard.

Governance and compliance

Not a vertical as such, but definitely should be, given the money-
making opportunities. Not-**** does not apply there as much as
it does not apply to a zillion other things, but hey, any port in a
storm, you know?

Mountains

Definitely vertical. Absolutely the most vertical thing you can
find, other than skyscrapers, of course. And rockets, they are
mostly vertical, unless launched by the EC. Poles. Telegraph poles
that is, not the Eastern European chapters of itSMF; they are
definitely vertical. And trees. And lots of people who are not in
the entertainment industry are vertical too, though a significant
proportion in the Netherlands are horizontal. Allegedly. Ask Ivo.
It was his 40th birthday and he chose the venue.

But how does '****' or indeed Not-**** apply? Well, we didn't
think you would ask, just take the whole thing on trust really,
but now that you have asked ... er, well it is explained that, well,
you plan to go up a mountain. Or maybe down, it doesn't matter
really. Except you couldn't go down unless you were already up;
that is known as a space-time parallax erm, thingy-wotsit ... and
then, you measure how you will demonstrate success, most likely
by being able to take a picture at the top, then you can review
what went wrong (losing your team in the crevasse was maybe
not a good thing, though I suppose that depends on who they
were), and plan to do things differently next time (take a ski lift
perhaps, or more alcohol and some decent sandwiches on the
way). And then do it again since everything has to be repeatable.
And then do it again since everything has to be repeatable.

And then do it again since everything has to be repeatable.

And then do it again since everything has to be repeatable.

Technoids
We told you Technoids do not apply. Either to '****' or Not-****.

Sport
High performance teams use Not-**** in their training regimes. The mighty Manchester United ruled the English Premier League until they lost the plot, failing to manage incidents (the Best Carry Out, the Cantona Kick, the Beckham Whinge, the Goalkeeping Crisis) which ultimately led to known errors that, frankly, they did nothing about. Incidentally, all of these are now cocktails that can be purchased at the bar in the executive suite at Old Trafford. Though they are obviously repackaged every season into trendy new glasses, just so they can charge you more.

Meanwhile Chelsea hired world-renowned '****' authors such as Frank Lampard and Claude Makelele and, of course, Joe Cole. These talents were enough to take Chelsea to the title, and Lampard is currently working on a new volume, 'Investing dubious millions in times of radical greed'.

Shipping
It is truly a miracle that the shipping lines of the world run entirely on '****' guidelines. Small ships are, of course, different to big ships and have to be steered differently. As for navigation, well, how can it possibly be the same? So a purpose-built version is now available to illustrate the huge, huge differences. Not that there are any, of course.

Computing and High Technology
Absolutely nothing applies to this sector. Except, of course '****'; the most important industry needs the most opportunities to exploit its paymasters. And a frequently-asked question is 'Where do I start?' usually followed up with 'I have no brain; provide me with a template or I will be unable to write:

- a business plan
- a service level agreement
- a business continuity plan (see 'Levee support and guidance')
- an IT contingency plan
- anything that requires me to think
- my name' (not as extreme as you may think if the idiot is incapable of any other writing activity).

Blogs
A major new development since IT Service Management from Hell V2. As in most upgrades, this new feature serves absolutely no useful purpose whatsoever.

Except to demonstrate the sad fact that everyone thinks they are unique and that what they have to say is actually interesting. Despite lots of evidence to the contrary ... people still think that blogs are interesting ...

Actually blogs are a big threat, and not in the way you think. It's a known fact that aliens tuned in to the planet Earth ether and unfortunately missed the important part (like 'hello', 'do come for a nice cup of tea' and 'would you like a Custard Cream with that?') because they were swamped by the millions of ranting blogs out there. Promptly labeling the place as the Psychotic Ward of the Galaxy, we've been dumped with all the oddballs within a 152 light-year radius. Think about it. Cloning luminescent pigs? Nobody sane could have thought that one up. Certain Presidents we could mention? – that vacant look is now explained. Whacko? Well, hands up who hadn't spotted that one.

How what does IT *Service Management from Hell* advise on blogs? Should we all go and get a life? Absolutely not –V3 wants more and more blogging. Anything that makes us all more dependent on IT means more development and more upgrades and more money for this particular problem. So bring it on.

7.2 Documentation Release for Industry Sectors

As a result of the consultation in the previous chapter, the following titles in the IT Service Management from Hell series are being withdrawn and revised in order to update some of the ever-so-slight issues that beset them, such as being crap, written by us instead of by experts and generally being a waste of printers ink and paper. (Yes, all those trees have died in vain...)

IT Service Management from Hell's Guide to Managing Nuclear Reactors

Without for one minute admitting that this book was, er, rubbish or admitting any liability for sheep that glow in the dark, we do concede that we were, perhaps, overstretching when we decided to upgrade our documented best practice on running nuclear reactors. Looking on the bright side, Chernobyl would not now be famous if they had not followed our best practice and, as for Three Mile Island, well, it's not as if it were someplace important like a heavily populated part of the USA .

Oh, it is in the USA?

Well, well, you learn something new every day.

Could this explain the re-election of George Bush? (Hurrah! The fog lifts ...)

And another thing: if you really need someone to write a nice 'template' for a business continuity plan rather than create one for yourself, perhaps you should resign from 'management' and go answer a phone somewhere. (But preferably not at my bank/ insurance broker/accountant.)

Tiger Management – A Management Guide

A big 'hello' to Siegfried and Roy, and just a little reminder that you cannot sue the British Crown guys. No matter what guidance you followed, the responsibility is yours. We understand, your Las Vegas enterprise may well have lost millions since those tiger teeth collided with the spongy bits in your neck Mr. Roy, but really, you cannot blame me or Paul. Or even the tiger for that matter; he just needed a nibble. If you want to be picky, ok we admit, we didn't actually study tigers out in India, but we definitely were aware of someone who did and that enabled us to write the book.

Many of our contributors actually read books on the subject and at least one has a collection of Tigger toys, so get over it. And get well soon! Oh, and don't do it again – for one thing, it traumatized the audience no end.

Farm Management in Zimbabwe – A Pocket Guide

Now you cannot blame us for this one. How were we to know when that nice president of theirs offered us a vast sum of money to get our logo on this module, that, in fact, he knew even less about farming than we did?

Communist State Maintenance and Improvement – A Manifesto

Again, not guilty. Some very nice gentlemen from the CIA claimed to know all about initiatives to maintain and improve communism, and presented us with a very large amount of money in a nice red box. Of course, we mean a project plan.

That all expenses-paid excursion to Virginia to discuss in detail, over no more than two or three dozen bottles of wine that we put on the expense account, had no bearing on our decision. And in fact, we would do it again. Or not.

Levee support and guidance – an Extremely Small Pocket Guide with a print run of 10 copies

Now this one was not as bad as all that, after all it only affected poor people, so no harm done. And according to many experts in other standards and frameworks. New Orleans was no one's fault because the city was entirely populated by deviants and/or poor people, or poor people. Did we mention the poor people?

And be fair, what other levees have given way as a result of Not-****? Name one? Hah!

IT Service Management from Hell in SITU

We will be republishing this book very soon. When it was written we had been telling the world that Not-**** applied to any size of IT organization; then we had a brainwave. We would publish a book about Not-**** in Small IT Units and get royalties anyway. We admit, we didn't immediately spot the contradiction of publishing a book specifically about small IT units when we had been so careful to keep everyone informed that the library was applicable no matter what and irrespective of business.

Incidentally we hope to pull-off a similar trick when we pretend that Not-**** is actually different in 'industry verticals' see section 7.1.

IT service Management from Hell and the Goblet of Fire

We did not rip-off JK Rowling. No indeed. Paul has, in fact, been selling signed limited edition cartoons of the Goblet of Fire for some weeks now and, in fact, discovered the chamber of secrets, carving his initials into the hindquarters of the basilisk when it was not looking.

Well, he had to, of course. That is, do it while it was not looking, otherwise he wouldn't be here would he? Actually, now that we come to think of it, he hasn't moved for a week or two; we just put that down to the pharmaceuticals though …

IT Service Management from Hell and Fashion – in Full Colour and Black (which is always in)

We bow to our superiors. We upgrade *IT Service Management for Hell* once every three years and find this fraud frankly embarrassing. But the fashion industry upgrade clothes once every three months and don't seem to have a problem with it. Every twelve weeks they persuade half the global population to ditch perfectly serviceable items of clothing and buy something which frankly makes even the leggiest model look quite ridiculous. But what the hell; if it makes money, who are we to have principles? IT service Management from Hell V4 will tackle this upgrade market and ensure that all computers change this season's colours (and I'm sorry silver or metallic will no longer be the 'new black'). Docking stations will now be available in either stiletto or wedge format. And for all those who regularly lose their Bluetooth gadget, a Plunging Neckline will become 'de rigueur'. For men, we are advised that 'single-breasted' or 'double breasted' will not be an issue – mostly because we aren't allowed to use terms like that in today's egalitarian society (there you go Sharon … we complied at least once). We will be changing colours of laptop back-packs and carriers once every six months and we're going to make sure that they carry the latest in 'bling'. For those who want to know, Spring 2007 will be Burberry check, with diamante 'references'.

Adaptors

The IT Service Management from Hell Editors are offering a prize of US$ 1 million to anyone who can invent an adaptor that fits all appliances. In terms of the most frustrating things on the planet this issue ranks as high as Jaguar never relaunching the XK150 Roadster. Or trying to find a German with a sense of humour.

Annexes – a.k.a. the redundant bits

It is imperative in any upgrade to leave in a tremendous amount of redundant garbage that has no purpose of functionality at all. After all God filled the human genome with redundant material and who are we to argue with the greatest Upgrader of them all?

Our redundant material is attached here. It has no specific purpose at all.

The key thing with redundant software (or even genes) is that it will really let you down at a really important time. This is usually when you should be working on a hyper-critical delivery and your boss catches you reading this instead......

Appendix A: Not-**** Foundation Examination – Test Questions

The most useful appendix to any book ever: Not-** Foundation certificate exam**

Service Desk Module
What is the objective of the Service Desk?
- To insult the users when they phone up
- To listen to the users and pretend that we care about their concerns, to promise to give priority to their requests and then do nothing about it
- To provide a single point of contact for users where they can receive polite, professional, service focused treatment from us

Incident Management
What is the objective of Incident Management?
- To annoy users
- To keep track of difficult users so that the IT organization can take measures to bring them into line
- To provide a place where users can quite rightly complain about the atrocious levels of service they receive from us

Problem Management
What is the objective of Problem Management?
- To develop and create interesting problems and distribute these to users
- To 'pro-actively' take measures to bring difficult users under control
- To try to identify and remove the problems and known errors that we have, through our incompetence and carelessness inflicted upon the user community

Change Management
This module is still under 'change management'
In other words it hasn't yet been built. Considering how successful most IT change projects are (in terms of delivering on time), don't hold your breath.

Configuration Management
Which of the following is Configuration Management?
- It allows us to put stickers and numbers on PCs to make users think we are professional
- To allow the Help Desk to annoy users by asking them to try to locate a number hidden somewhere on their PC
- to have to quote long codes every time they want to register an incident – e.g. PCa:1245/35/room5/userxBc: qF12bB (ensuring they correctly quote capitals and non capitals)

- It allows us to keep track of the infrastructure components and to be able to efficiently and effectively perform changes and resolve problems … (as if we care).

Release Management
Which of the following is a Release Management activity?
- To download viruses onto user PCs
- To ensure that the latest bugs and known errors are distributed to all PCs
- To ensure that original versions of authorized software are safely stored.

Service Level Management
Which of the following items should be included in service level agreements?
- Threats of physical violence to users exceeding agreed levels of service
- Complicated algorithms that explain how 'availability' is calculated
- Penalty clauses so that the user community can punish us for yet again failing miserably to meet their service level requirements.

Financial Management
This module isn't finished yet.
We hope to have this module up and running soon. We simply didn't have enough money to pay for the development.

Capacity Management
What is the objective of Capacity Management?
- To carefully balance and optimize workloads to such an extent that an IT 'Gridlock' occurs
- To ensure that comment 'a short wait will occur' message appears followed by the system hanging up whenever a user starts a crucial transaction
- To ensure that user capacity and performance demands can be optimally achieved and in a cost efficient way.

Availability Management
This module isn't available yet. (Joke! Gettit??)
We hope to have this module up and running soon (This comes from an IT specialist – work it out for yourself!)

Continuity Planning

What is the objective of the Business Continuity Management?

- To ensure that IT will survive any disaster inflicted upon it by the business
- To take measures to ensure that disasters and calamities regularly impact business continuity
- To ensure that we in IT take measures to guarantee business continuity in the event of any disaster impacting IT.

Security Management

I'm sorry, but you are not authorized to use this module.
We hope to have this module up and running soon ...

Appendix B: Other standards and frameworks

As the most hyped framework in the world, that is, in fact, not any kind of a standard and has been specifically mentioned as not being strictly necessary to what is a standard, Not-****** does therefore fit in well with other frameworks, standards and reference models.

B.1 Kabbalah
Madonna herself has provided the mapping for Not-**** and Kabbalah. Taking time out from her world record breaking grab-your-crotch-and money tour, she has documented a clear and concise mapping of her own version of Kabbalah with Not-**** to illustrate that she can do what tons of others have been doing for years.

B.2 Intelligent Design
Working with teams of biblical experts, we have established without doubt that Not-**** is proof of Intelligent Design. This new mapping, as rigorously determined as 'the Mariachi Code' or the 'DaVinci Papers' or even the best selling 'Shroud of Turin Book of Excuses for Throwing Out Carbon Dating', has now been published in a form totally useless to the average person thus enabling our Consultants to make a pile of money.

B.3 Scientology
We asked Tom Cruise to map Not **** to Scientology but he was not available. John Travolta however kindly stepped forward and his dance steps for the mapping can be downloaded from:

www.vanharen.net

For a considerable amount of money blow-up inflatable dolls of Uma Thurman are also available from Van Halen Publishing.

B.4 ISO 17799
Not **** maps to this standard marginally better than '****'.

B.4 The White Album
We think this is clearly a standard and a milestone in Rock History.

It is another well known fact that if 'Dear Prudence' is played backwards at 78 rpm, the authors can clearly be heard mapping all past and future lyrics to Not-****. In the background those with discerning hearing will make out the words 'Kill yourselves before it is too late, Van Haren is the devil, there is only one true '****''. Speculation that one of the early prophets somehow blagged their way into the sessions has never been ratified.

B.5 Rap
With its rampant sexism and intrinsic violent prose, even the most superficial reading of Not **** will enable a clear mapping to be undertaken.

B.6 Basel II
Like a glove.

B.7 KOBITT
Why on Earth would anyone in their right mind map to this unless they see the opportunity to make mountains of cash from the unwary. Oh, wait a minute ...

B.8 The Geneva Convention
Yes. Even in America.

B.9 The Constitution of the USA
Dead easy.

B.10 HIPPA
Yep, that one as well.

B.11 HIPPApotamus
You don't catch us out that easy. And anyway yes.

B.12 PRINCE2
No, sorry. If '****' does not map to it how can we.

Appendix C: Communications planning

C.1   Spokespeople

Get a rock star to front your communications planning. Rock stars are cheap so long as there is a Pope or two to meet or maybe a President and of course both Popes and Presidents (and even Prime Ministers) just love the opportunity to be seen as 'right on' and 'hip' to 'the kids'.

Rock stars are also so well-educated and well-read that they have opinions that need to be heard (and acted upon) on everything, making them ideal for an '****' project. Imagine the credibility that Boy George or the mighty Sting will bring to your Capacity Management planning. The insight of the poet and philosopher Bono, whose every utterance is considered as Holy Writ. Or Lord (as surely he will be) Geldof, who can with a single swearword get management off your back.

C.2   Communities of interest

Tie a piece of string around the wrist of every person in your team. This will bind them to you in an eternal cosmological cradle of inter-dimensional blessings. If you can afford rubber bands even better; your team will appreciate the investment and go forth and sing of the great things that surely will be. Teach your team to go about their business smiling and with bright shining eyes (no one smiles in '****' projects imagine how unnerving that will be for the opposition---erm, that is the unconverted we mean).

Write a team song along the lines of:

The ** Foundation Song**
*Amazing '****', how sweet thou art*
That saved an IT wretch like me
I once was a human but now am mutated
And boring for all to see.

And be sure that your posse applauds mightily whenever the '****' word is spoken. It is often useful to adopt a serene, utterly becalmed almost dreamlike demeanor when your '****' project is discussed. No one ever is calm in reality and people will think you belong to a mysterious (and dangerous) cult. Not far from the truth really.

And don't forget, this is still the town of **** we are writing about …

Appendix D: Terminology

'****' version 3 will also be introducing a 'new' set of '****' terminology so we thought we would also produce one, to help readers play bullshit bingo. We will provide a set of words that version 3 adherents will use when trying to flog you … er convince you … about why 'their' **** version 3 will help you. If you hear a Version 3 follower use three or more of these words or phrases within one minute you can shout "Bull-shit bingo".

ASL	Misspelling of the name of the head of Application management as referred to by business managers "What an absolute ASL".
Service lifecycle	Because IT organizations are so piss-poor at providing services and the fact that new IT systems are usually withdrawn from live use within a short period of introduction, this tends to be noticed by the business. Therefore we use the term *lifecycle* (as opposed to the gargling death throws of IT systems spluttering their last bleeps). We now say the service has reached the end of its *lifecycle*, a perfectly natural process.
Portfolio management	This generally means wallet-management, it means the business should open its portfolio (wallet) and pour the entire contents into IT so that we can build more innovative IT solutions that we can phase out of their service *lifecycle* before anybody even new they were actually in live use.
IT Governance	A new way for large accounting firms to make even more money from the business by putting the fear of the Almighty into the CEO that ICT will be his or her downfall, it will all end up in tears and the CEO will end up in prison and IT all live happily ever after.
Business value	Something that goes down exponentially with each $ or Euro invested in IT.
FISM	Fellow of the Institute of Service Managers. A bit like the fellowship of the ring only totally different. Generally reckoned to be a race-memory of those early consultancy get-togethers where grunting was an art form and audiences too stupid to do anything other than listen in awe. Before rushing to join, remember Groucho's famous and apt remark about not wishing to be a member of any club that wanted him to join. One really good benefit of membership however is that you can guarantee that when the plum jobs come up you will be first in line irrespective of your suitability. And you will be able to bask in self-congratulation and indeed the guaranteed congratulations of your cronies. Peers. That should have been peers. I mean, why else have such a club? It is quite proper you know.

Babel FISM	Misspelling. It should be babel FISH. A small fish that when placed in the ear would allow people to understand any language that was spoken even '****' V3 from a FISMer.
Babble FISM	Not a spelling mistake. This is something many FISMs do all the time. Babble on endlessly about the benefits of service management and how it will facilitate world peace, remove starvation from the world and solve AIDS (Atrocious IT Delivery of Services).
Business Case	This is when the business expects us to specify the business value of an IT investment. They are no longer happy with 'A really sexy looking IT system that hums ever so softly and look at those cool green lamps that glow when you switch the lights off'.

Appendix E: The Adams families

Let us investigate the connections between the various Ad(d)ams families. It has nothing to do with the book, but provides a change of style and at least a spark of innovation---unlike version three of course. Starting with the legend that is Douglas; go and buy all of his books and wonder.

Douglas Adams

Incredibly, and untruthfully, Douglas, of course, based every ludicrous situation on the itSMF, the 'InTergalactic Service Management Forum'. Unfortunately for diplomacy and the rest of the human race, this group won the space race and has set up Chapters throughout the universe. Activities are limited to booking conference calls at a bad time for everyone – and if you thought that Global conference calls were bad, just think what it's like when you take Einstein-ian physics into account. Space and time laws means that conversations have been set-up with the Publishing Chairwoman's grandmother on several occasions and this explains why itSMF is now supporting titles on 'Homemade Apple Pie in IT' and 'Implementing Best Practice Linen Cleaning'.

Little known true fact: National Towel Day is an annual event held each 25th May, to celebrate the life of our great and sorely-missed Guru. Significantly, the date is of NO significance whatsoever …

Scott Adams

A living legend (and long may that continue) whose cartoon strips do not satirize corporate life. They ARE corporate life. It is a not well-known fact, that is, of course, not a fact, that all of Scott's ideas are based on actual happenings in the Office of Galactic Commerce. How the OGC came to inherit **** is an illustration that karma is not always reliable.

Brian Adams

Even more tenuously linked to this chapter is famed Canadian rocker Brian. Blessed (*no, not Brian Blessed, Brian Adams, you fool! Ed.*) with boring songs and a basically, inadequate haircut, Brian is famous for not answering the question 'Did you shag her then?', leaving it up to others to claim that he did and thereby be a man to be admired.

This is marginally less loathsome than the stance of the ginger hooray who not only tells the world that yes, he did shag her and more than once too, despite being ginger and a bit of a ponce, but much more loathsome than simply saying no.

The Addams Family

Long time OGC watchers will recognize the gothic characters in the family; Tony Ad(d)ams for example, left Arsenal to move to a more exciting career in OGC and ended up on the booze and engaged to an exotic dancer from Wolverhampton. He failed to write anything of note. Uncle Fester Addams carried on a career of unwavering bitterness and unswerving dedication to carrying around chips for both shoulders, telling anyone who would listen that he had been misunderstood.

Gomez and Morticia are still to be seen on moonless nights in exotic Norwich UK, rattling chains and demanding licence money.

Endive Adams (founder of Vegiality in the Garden of Eden)

The legend of Adam and Eve is, in fact, an urban myth born of real events. A past **** prophet, Endive loved vegetables. And by that, we mean he loved them. In the Biblical sense. Nothing wrong with that, of course. Khazariawa is a big place (not as big as a galaxy of course, but pretty big nonetheless) and everyone has a kink somewhere. Ask around.

Anyway, Endive founded a sect based on his love of vegetables, and pretty soon (**** being one of those places where not much happens unless linked to the sex industry), he gathered together a set of disciples who terrorized the local vegetables, many of which were sentient and therefore quite capable of being a little discombobulated by unwelcome fondling of the florets or the odd grope around the root.

Turnips were molested; carrots were subject to miscegenation (whatever that is); cauliflowers were, well, let's be blunt here, felt up. And as for corn cobs, you don't want to know where they went.

We said you don't want to know.

The upshot was that Endive had to undergo treatment at the famous Perversion Aversion Institute, where he was introduced to fruit as a means to wean him off the veggies. An unfortunate incident (that later became a problem ... and eventually a change, ... erm, and then a release ...) with a banana ... led to Endive being banished to ASL, an uninhabited plain near ****, where his perversions could be managed.

As the inhabitants of **** were infamous for their ability to write history in precise accordance with things they wanted people not to know, it was decided that to eradicate all evidence of Vegiality, Endive would have to become a man of a more salubrious history. Over many years a legend was created where a mate was introduced called 'Eve' and 'Endive Adams' entries everywhere became corrupted to read Adams and Eve. Soon, the legend of Adam and Eve was created and a link made to the evil power of fruit to ensure that Vegiality would be consigned to history.

Samuel Adams

A world famous (in the USA) drink and once part of the history of the USA before he became a drink. Also famous for inventing the game show "Ye Blocke Busters".

Other titles recommended by the IT Service Management from Hell series:

Service Management: Companion volumes – what the critics say …

IT Procurement

Buying IT? Well, procurement is a real career killer if I ever saw one. Guaranteed that no one will give you a decent spec, and by the time the product with assorted applications has been delivered, your organization will have realigned its strategic direction. The product you've just acquired was for a telecommunications function and is no longer relevant for the new shoe manufacturing strategy. And neither are you.

So get this book pronto. Technically it is an end to end process which makes sure that all the correct boxes have been ticked and the purchasing process is efficient and cost-effective. But we all really know that it's about making you sure that you've got the correct documentation so that the buck doesn't stop with you. Become a procurement tyrant; you know that you want to.

Foundations of IT Service Management based on ****®

If you thought concrete was only needed as overshoes for Italian-American tough guys, think again. Without concrete your ITSM is nothing. Nada. Zip. Zilch. Less than zero. This book will take you through the pain of being certified to operate mechanical digging devices, the precise proportions of sand, gravel, cement and water needed to mix that just-so consistency and, of course, the best way to ice those pesky customers that you will be strategically placing in the trenches you learn to excavate. Get it before they get you.

Service CMM (*I still don't know what this is about. Ed.*)

Ready to impress the neighbors? Get to grips with the only best practice that can wash whiter than white AND extract boy scouts from horses hooves. Yes, the Service CMM, so good even Albert Einstein wanted one and, in fact, predicted the existence of one before it ever actually existed. Learn about, well, services. And yes CMM. How can you lose? Be the first one in your neighborhood to go nuclear. Or service. And please do tell us what the thing is about.

Implementing Guide (HDI)

Implementing service support? This is guaranteed. Take a six ounce piece of support and whack it, fairly indiscriminately it must be said, around what might indeed be an ear, and there you have it. Implementation. If only all so-called implementation guides were so simple and dependable. This does exactly what is says on the tin. Cover. We mean cover. It implements. Yeah. Right on.

Project Management: An Introduction based on PRINCE2

Ah, a personal favorite. Did you know that this, the most famous project management method known to the galaxy, was actually the project management method formerly known as PRINCE? Now enhanced with a '2', this method was conceived, written, performed and actually delivered … a year later than the project plan. But that was a PRINCE project plan and this one has '2'. It is well recognized as number 2 in toilets throughout the galaxy and only here can you purchase the odor-free version.

Manage people. Places. Time. Money. Women. Yes, women. We are not saying this to attract men to buy this. Well, yes we are. But let's face it, men are so gullible. So buy this book and women will be on-tap. Or if you are a woman, buy this book because as you can see we are smart enough to understand men so it must be good.

ASL

As a friend of mine once so pithily put it (and he was able to pith anywhere), you need to be a right ASL to love this. Applications. Services. And yes, that letter made famous, no, indispensable, by ITI … I speak of 'L'. Whatever the 'L' that is. But there are a lot of them. And we have all of them. Or ALL of them. If you can have LL. Be cool like cool J. He was nothing without his LL.

No, it is not medication; we are just a little hyper after all the Dutch coffee. That we erm, drank in the brown cafes.

Please buy this book. The authors need you. We need you. 10% of all proceeds go directly to us. At least we are honest.

BISL

Wittgenstein and Kant are just two of the philosophers who were smart enough to have nothing to do with this stuff. Oscar Wilde (briefly) left Alfred to read this before writing 'The Importance of Being Earnest'. It is rumored that Gurdjieff himself read the rubbish, and this why Kate Bush is so weird. Nevertheless, if you have a BISL fetish, only this will suffice. Business. Information Systems. And L. What more could you need?

CobiT and Governance

Fun with Dick and Jane? Well, Enron certainly dicked the public. So did Jane, but that's another story. Get a couple of grams of this in the rolled up Euro bill and your company will laugh in the face of government legislation and smack the pimpled bottom of auditors everywhere. Focused on being compliant and subservient (get back Monica …), this book has it all. Well, if not all, enough. If not enough, something. And COBIT. Like caballah sometimes spelled with a K. You can be cured of CobiT, or kobit, and we tell you how. You were not born CobiT; that is a myth created by the CobiT Liberation Movement. There is a CobiT mafia in TV and entertainment. Particularly in TV ... Do not worry. Electro-convulsive therapy is guaranteed to return you to normal. After this, you will return to the straight and narrow and consign BroKobit Mountain to the second hand (oo-er missus) store.

Cobbit auditor

PMS Group

The Not **** team has outsourced protection of its trademarked IP to PMS Group led by celebrity chief Pharoah Sanders. PMS currently exploits the copyright, that should read 'protects the copyright' of all of the IP produced by the Not **** owners, an arrangement that has worked well in swelling our coffers and with the added advantage of royally naffing-off some individuals who really do need to get over themselves.

PMS will each month get shirty with anyone they choose. Under the benevolent hand of Not-ITIL trademark owners, Pharoah Sanders will pull the rug out from under anyone who talks or writes about the method that dares to speak its name (unlike ****, a method that dare not speak its name for fear of, well, erm, similar things really).

The publishers do not want to create any confusion about the roles of 'Not ****', a worst practice method with adherents in every IT organization in the galaxy and '****' the method that dare not speak its name, with adherents only in Madrassahs run by itSMF, the organization that dare not speak the name of the method that dares not speak its name, in the event that the galaxy discovers that they have been excommunicated from the method.

This method (not that method, the other one) is administered by APM Group, led by a shadowy figure whose popularity in the UK has been compared to that of Ronaldo, a famous Portuguese-r and sporting gentleman.

Respected industry analyst Lefty Liebowitz interviewed the CEO of APMG about the role of all of the organizations that over many years have helped with building the brand and ubiquity of the method that dare not speak its name. What role did OGC set out for those trusted people, those died-in-the-wool supporters who endured hardship, deprivation and even mocking over their blind and unwavering devotion?

'None at all because they really don't give a flying one'.

And in the event of these loyal, nay, devoted followers suffering hardship?

'I think you may have mistaken OGC for an organization that cares'.

And what principal role would APMG play?

'Scapegoat'.

Publisher Ivo van Haren was interviewed about PMS in order to ensure that the differences between APMG and PMS were absolutely clear. Liebowitz first asked van Haren about the impact of PMS.

'Around half the population of the world will be members of PMS' he boasted, 'compared to a miniscule proportion in APMG. And what's more if you follow our method you'll find IT projects always deliver – on time and on budget. Because no one dares cross a person with PMS (certification). And that's the full story. Full stop. Period.'